Countryside Activity Book

Janet McKellar *and* Jenny Bullough

Illustrated by Jennifer Bailey

HIPPO BOOKS
SCHOLASTIC PUBLICATIONS LIMITED
LONDON

The Countryside Activity book is full of exciting things to make and do.
It includes activities with plants, animals and insects and explains the
changes which occur each month. You can keep a nature diary. Write down
each month some of the things you see, hear or feel. Then look back at it
at the end of the year.
Hidden on some double page spreads are four little creatures to be found;
spider; caterpillar; fly and ladybird. See if you can spot all of them.
At the top corner of each right hand page is a little picture. Flick the pages
over and you have a mini-book!

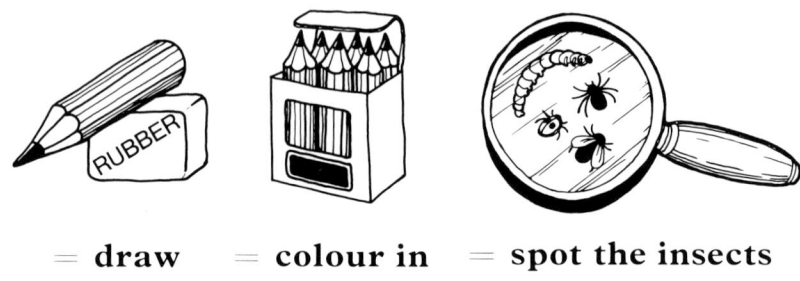

= **draw**　　= **colour in**　　= **spot the insects**

Scholastic Publications Ltd., 10 Earlham Street, London WC2H 9LN, England
Scholastic Inc., 730 Broadway, New York, NY10003, USA
Scholastic Tab Publications Ltd., 123 Newkirk Road, Richmond Hill, Ontario L4C 3G5, Canada
Ashton Scholastic Pty. Ltd., P.O. Box 579, Gosford, New South Wales, Australia
Ashton Scholastic Ltd., 165 Marau Road, Panmure, Auckland, New Zealand

This book conceived and designed by Beanstalk Books Ltd,
89 Park Hill, London SW4 9NX.
Text © 1987 Beanstalk Books Ltd.
Illustrations © 1987 Beanstalk Books Ltd.
First published in the UK by Scholastic Publications Ltd. 1987.

Printed in Hong Kong by Everbest
ISBN 0 590 70560 1

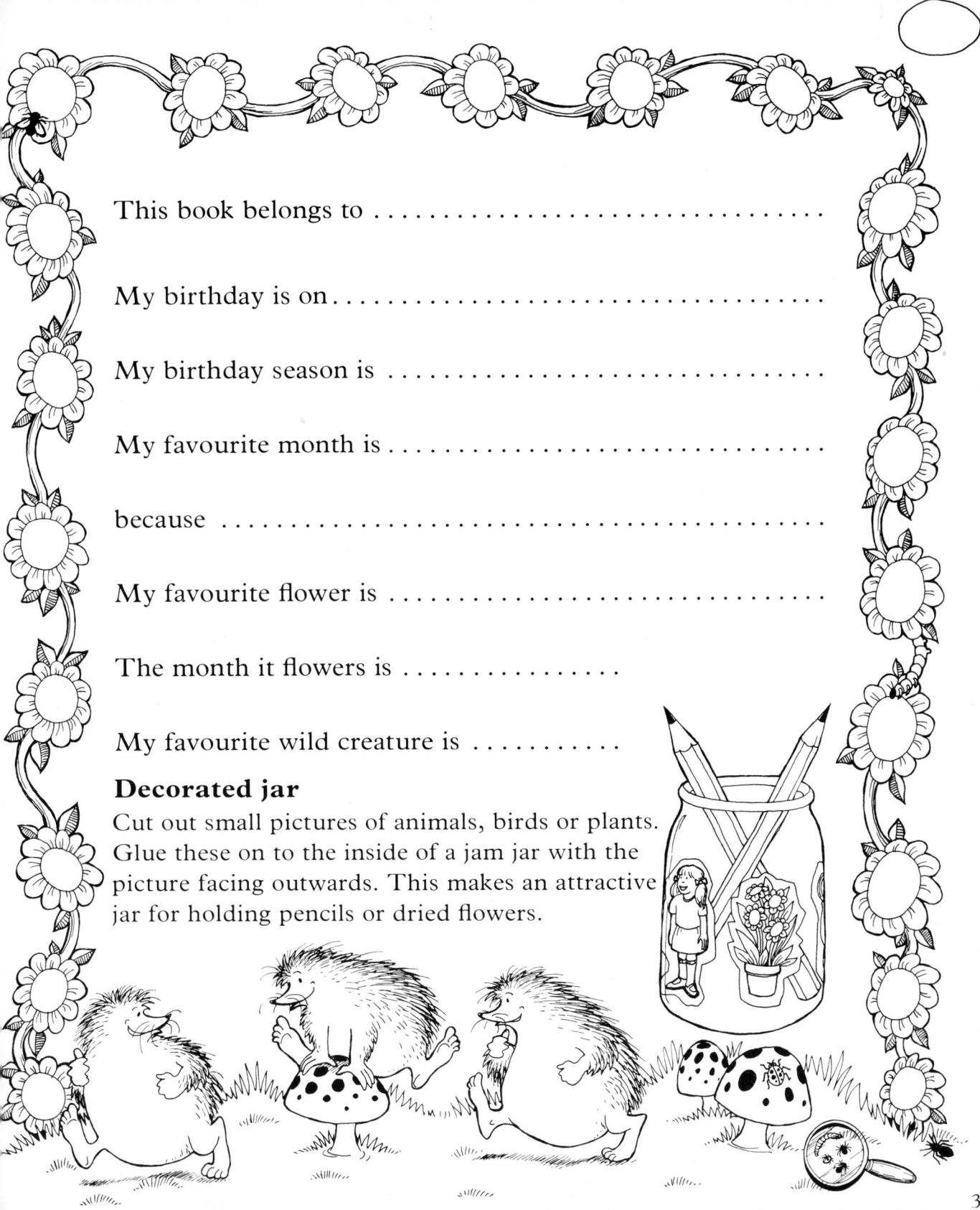

This book belongs to ....

My birthday is on..................................

My birthday season is ....

My favourite month is ....

because ....

My favourite flower is ....

The month it flowers is ....

My favourite wild creature is ....

Decorated jar

Cut out small pictures of animals, birds or plants. Glue these on to the inside of a jam jar with the picture facing outwards. This makes an attractive jar for holding pencils or dried flowers.

January

In January the days are short and the sun is low in the sky. It is often the coldest month of the year. The animals who are not asleep spend most of their time hunting for food.

Can you name the birds in the picture?
Answers at the bottom of the page.

Keep a record of the birds you can see on your bird-table. What food are they eating?

You can help the birds survive the winter by putting out food for them. Here are some suggestions.

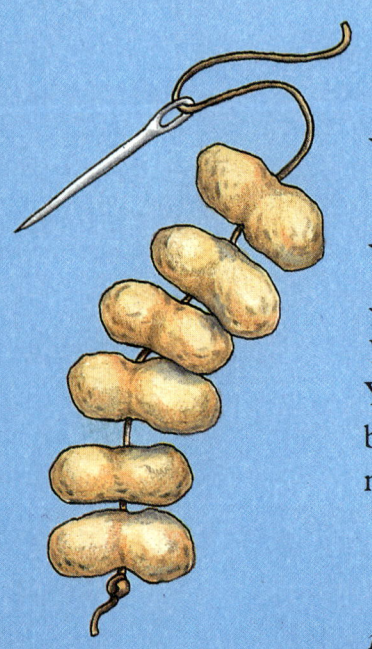

★ Thread peanuts on a string and hang them up.
Never put out salted nuts for birds.

★ Put out fresh water each day.

★ Make a bird cake.
You will need :
Yoghurt carton; match-stick; thin string; dried fruit; bread or cake crumbs; oatmeal; suet; cooked potato; melted fat *(ask an adult to help you with this)*.

Answers 1 blackbird 2 thrush 3 robin 4 blue tit 5 chaffinch 6 starling 7 house sparrow 8 great tit

4

Make the bell shown in the picture.

Mix the melted fat with the food
and pack into the yoghurt pot.
Leave to cool until set.
Hang up from a branch or bird-table.
Don't forget to put out bread and crumbs
on flat surfaces for the birds
that cannot hang upside down.

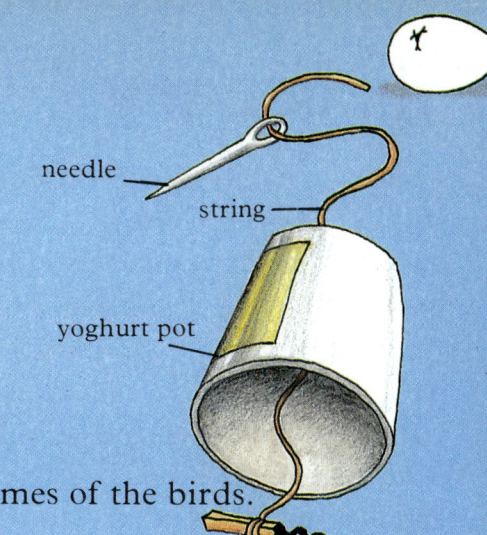

needle

string

yoghurt pot

match-stick

Fill in the dots with the missing letters to find the names of the birds.
Answers at the bottom of the page.

sp.rr.w	st.rl.ng	p.g..n
thr.sh	r.b.n	w..dp.ck.r
r..k	h.r.n	c.ck..

Thumb-print birds Turn the thumb-prints into birds.

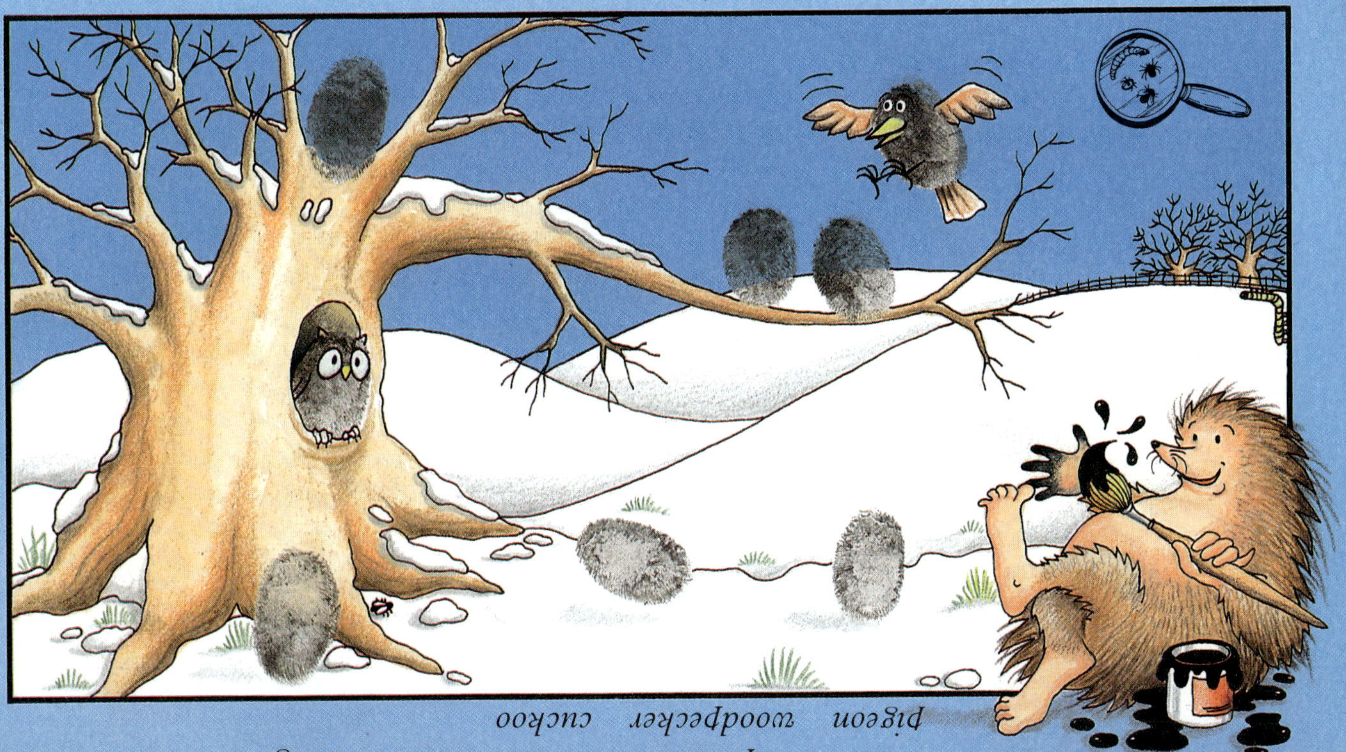

RUBBER

February

February is the shortest month and usually the wettest. The babies of many mammals will soon be born. Do you know what a mammal is? It is an animal with a backbone, its young are born alive and then fed on milk. Mammals need air to breathe and are warm-blooded. How many names of mammals can you find in the word square?

H	R	C	R	O	W	I	P	L	H	A	R	E
E	S	A	A	C	R	A	B	I	G	E	A	P
D	T	T	B	U	L	L	G	O	A	T	T	M
G	U	A	B	O	E	S	P	N	Ø	I	R	O
E	V	E	I	F	O	X	H	E	N	G	O	U
H	W	I	T	U	P	I	G	I	V	E	S	S
O	T	T	E	R	A	X	P	H	O	R	S	E
G	X	O	U	I	R	W	H	A	L	E	S	C
E	E	L	S	P	D	U	C	K	E	E	H	R
O	Y	I	T	V	O	L	C	A	N	O	A	O
W	Z	O	P	Z	G	S	O	A	K	I	R	W
L	S	N	A	K	E	O	W	A	S	P	K	M

Make a food chain

Food chains always begin with a plant.

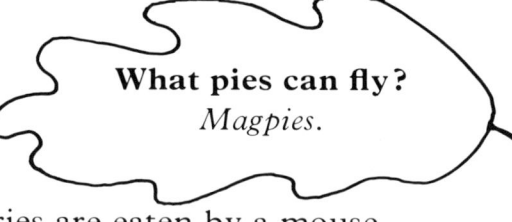

What pies can fly?
Magpies.

Berries are eaten by a mouse which may be eaten by a cat.

Complete the food chains

1  leaf

 caterpillar

 ?

2  grass

 ?

 fox

Answers   1 bird   2 rabbit

Match the tracks to the animals

1

3

4

2

7

5

6

March

In breezy March, the sun rises higher in the sky, the soil begins to warm up and the first signs of spring appear. If there are a few days of sunny weather, the frogs and toads will begin to lay their eggs.

Toadspawn tangle

Frogs lay their eggs in clumps. Toads lay theirs in long ropes. Can you unravel the tangle of ropes in the picture and find out which rope was laid by each toad?

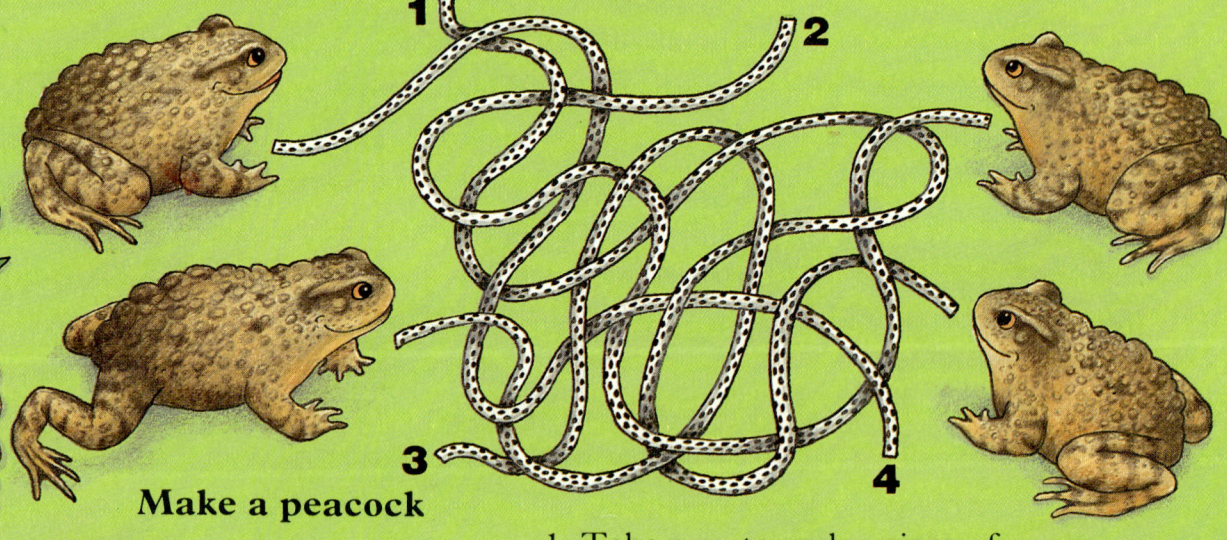

Make a peacock

1 Take a rectangular piece of paper 30 cm. × 20 cm. approximately. Draw oval shapes. Colour in using peacock colours: blue; mauve; yellow and turquoise.
2 Fold to form a fan.
3 Fold in half and secure at the top with a blob of glue.
4 Trace, cut out and colour the peacock shape.
5 Stick the peacock to the front of the fan tail with a blob of glue.

Water beetle game

Throw the correct numbers shown below for each part of the body and watch your beetle develop. You have to throw a 1 to start and draw the body. Feelers and eyes cannot be added until you have thrown a 2, which allows you to draw the head. Continue until complete.

Throw:

1 for the body
2 for the head
3 for each leg
4 for each eye
5 for each feeler

Gone fishing

Make your own fishing game. Either trace the freshwater creatures on to card or draw your own animals. Fix a paperclip at the head end. Make a rod out of a sheet of tightly rolled newspaper secured with sticky tape. Tie a magnet to a length of string and attach to the rod. Each creature has a number. Put them on a tray or plate for a pond and go fishing. The player who catches the highest score wins.

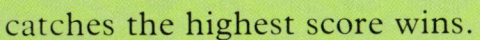

9

April

The days are much longer now. The birds sing loudly. Insects rouse themselves after the cold winter. They provide much-needed food for the egg-laying birds.

There are many different types of birds' nests which are built in a variety of places.

Can you find the right nest for each bird?

Make an edible birds' nest with marzipan eggs

Ask an adult to help you cook this.
You will need:
2 shredded wheat
100 grams cooking chocolate
100 grams marzipan
mixing bowl and spoon

What goes croak, croak, when it's misty?
A frog horn.

Tear up the shredded wheat into small pieces and put into the mixing bowl. Melt the chocolate over a low heat. Add to the shredded wheat. Using the spoon divide the mixture in two scoops to make two small nests and place on a greased baking tray. Using your fingers make into nest shapes. Mould the marzipan into egg shapes. Allow the nests to cool and harden and then place the eggs inside.

Make a bird mobile

Trace these shapes on to card.
Cut out, colour and hang them from
a wire coat hanger with thread.

magpie

house martin

jay

robin

May

Now that there are many insects around to help with pollination, plants can start to produce their flowers. Parks, gardens and the countryside are filled with activity.

Can you solve the flower crossword?

What is a caterpillar?
A worm in a fur coat.

Planting pips and seeds

Try planting orange, lemon or grapefruit pips.

Make a hole at the bottom of a yoghurt pot, put in a few stones then fill with soil. Plant two or three pips in the pot and cover with soil. Water regularly and in two or three weeks shoots will be seen. These plants will not bear fruit but make very attractive house plants. Transplant to a larger pot when the plant is about 10 cm. high.

Grow seeds on cotton wool.
Place a thin layer of cotton wool on the bottom of a polystyrene meat tray. Dampen the cotton wool. Sprinkle half a packet of mustard and cress seeds onto the dampened cotton wool. Place them on a window sill. Water daily and in a few days the seeds will be growing. In a week you will be able to make cress sandwiches!

Make a vivarium tank for mini beasts.
You will need a plastic sweet jar. Place on its side. Ask an adult to make holes in the lid. Put earth, stones and a variety of leaves on the bottom for food. Collect a few snails, wood lice and worms and place them in the jar. Replace the lid. Watch the mini beasts select between the different foods offered. Keep the mini beasts for two or three days only before returning them to the garden.

plastic sweet jar on its side – holes in lid

earth and stones to burrow in

June

June has the longest hours of daylight. Plants and animals are growing fast and with the long, sunny days and warm nights there is plenty of food for all.

Test your powers of observation. Look at this picture for about one minute and then turn to page 32 and see if you can answer the Mighty Memory questions.

Birds come in all shapes and sizes. They are adapted to where they live. Some have bright colours, some dull. Many water birds have webbed feet while birds of prey have talons and wading birds have long legs. Some birds have beaks that are long and thin, some are short and hooked. In the space below, design your own bird.

Name of bird. . . . . Date. . . . .

Discovered by. . . . . Where it lives. . . . .

July

July is a restful time for birds and animals, after the busy weeks of raising their young. Butterflies sip nectar from the summer flowers and the warm night air is filled with moths.

A game for four players.
You will need: a dice and shaker.

Trace these counters on to card. Cut out and colour each one a different colour.

START →

EGGS LAID
go on two squares 1

2

9

ATTACKED BY BIRDS!
hurry on two squares 8

7

6

10

LOSE YOUR WAY ON THE PATH
go back to beginning! 11

12

13

STOP TO GUZZLE IN VEGETABLE PATCH
miss one turn 14

22 HURRY TO SUITABLE SLEEPING PLACE go on three squares

23

ASLEEP IN CHRYSALIS miss two turns

ZZZZZZzz

21

24

25

20 LOOK FOR PLACE TO MAKE CHRYSALIS miss one turn

26 EMERGE FROM CHRYSALIS go on one square

GS 'CHING one turn

3

4

19

27

EAT LEAVES miss two turns

5

18

28 BUTTERFLY!

16

17 TRY TO ESCAPE HUNGRY HEDGEHOGS go on three squares

FINISH

August

The sun has warmed the earth and sea, the days are still long and it is holiday time. In the countryside the farmers are busy harvesting the corn.

Try this nature bingo when you next go on a long journey. Tick off the objects when you have seen them.

kestrel	river	pine tree	cow
holly tree	magpie	pub sign with bird	bird-table
pigeon	dog	seagull	oak tree

Make up your own nature bingo and write in things of special interest to you.

These well-known rhymes have lost their bird or animal. Can you fill in the blanks?

Baa baa black . . . .

A . . . . he would a-wooing go.

Three blind . . . .

The . . . . and the pussy cat.

One, two, three, four, five once I caught a . . . . alive.

Hicketty picketty my black . . . .

To market to market to buy a fat . . . .

Mary had a little . . . .   *Answers at the bottom of the page.*

Answers: sheep mice frog owl fish hen pig lamb

Sssssew a ssssock sssssnake

You will need :
old sock
two buttons for eyes
strip of felt for the tongue

1 Put the sock on your hand.
2 Wiggle your hand about and
   decide where to put the eyes.
3 Sew on the buttons.
4 Cut felt into strip
   with forked end.
5 Sew on tongue and see
   slippery Suzie slither!

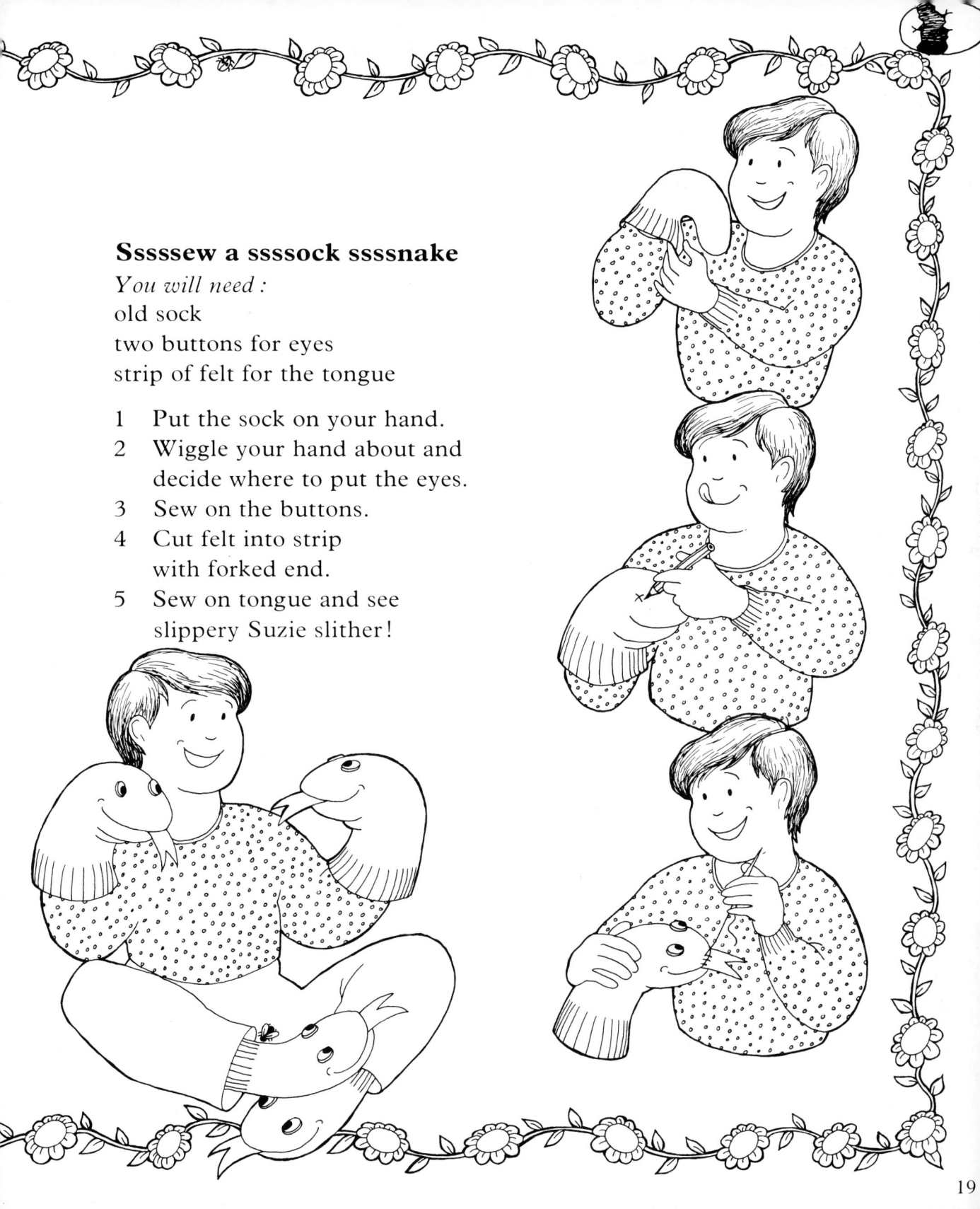

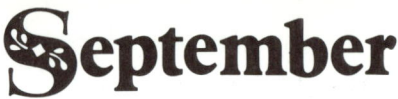

September

The first hint of autumn is in the air. The trees and hedgerows are heavy with the fruit which will help to feed the animals through the winter. Although still warm the days are getting shorter.

Tree identification puzzle

Below you will find five outlines of trees and five words with the letters jumbled up. Sort out the correct name of the tree and write it beside the right outline. *Answers at the bottom of the page.*

1 LARPOP 2 SOCST EINP 3 KAO 4 MLE 5 CHRAL

Make a Nature Trail around the area where you live. Draw a map for your friends to follow.

Answers 1 *oak* 2 *larch* 3 *poplar* 4 *Scots pine* 5 *elm*

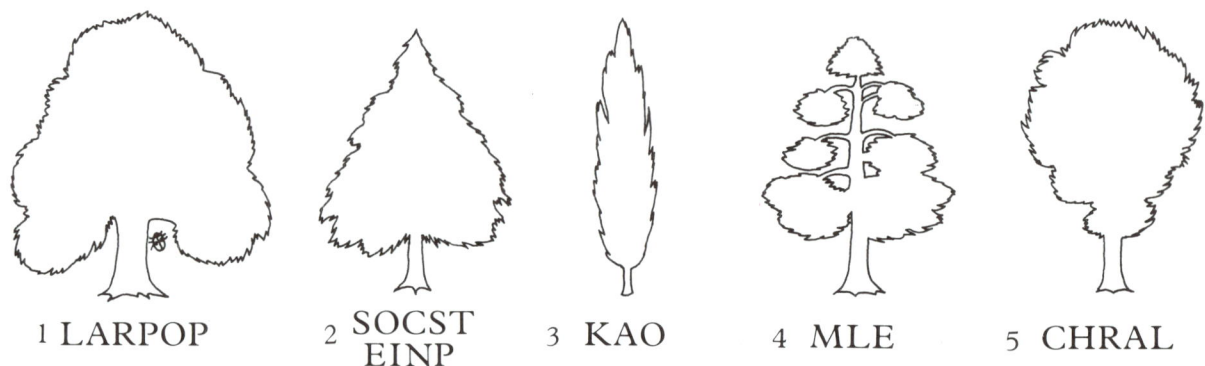

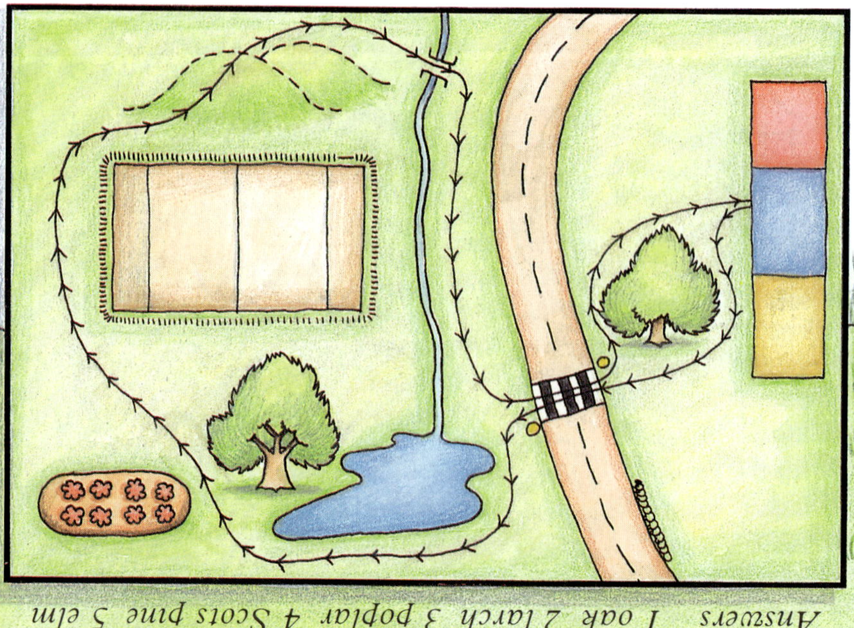

Look carefully at the trees near where you live. They provide a home for many different animals, insects and birds. Draw some of them in and around this tree.

October

The last of the summer visiting birds has left for warmer lands and from the north the first winter visitors appear. The shortening days put a chill in the air and the animals fatten themselves up for winter.

Creatures of the night

Badgers, owls, bats, hedgehogs, foxes and moths are creatures of the night. Can you guide the animals to their homes in the moonlight? See picture. *Answers at the bottom of the page.*

Game

You will need two tiddlywinks and two players. Press one counter on to the other to make it jump. Try to make it land on one of the animals below. Have ten flicks then add up your score.

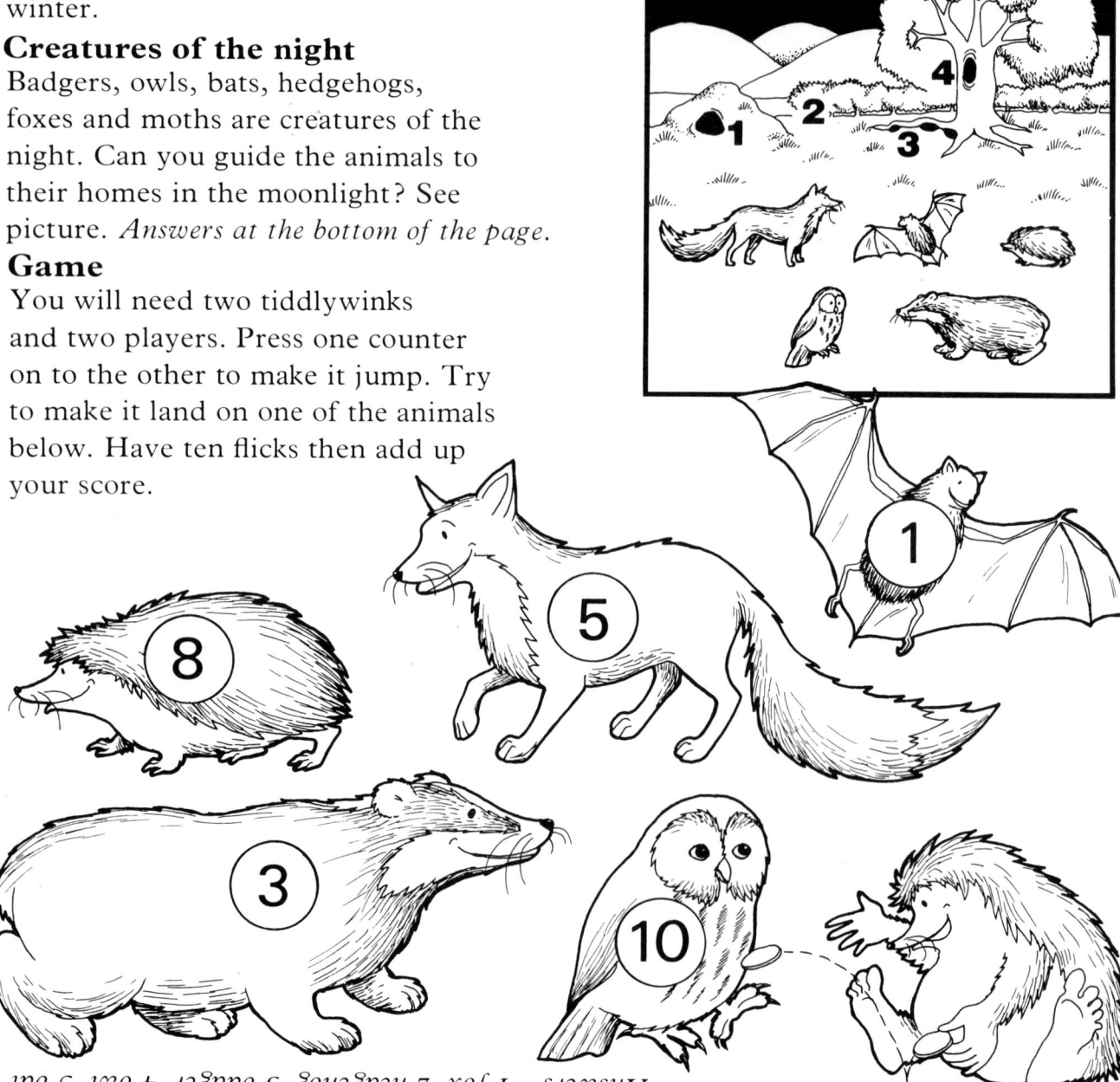

Answers 1 fox 2 hedgehog 3 badger 4 owl 5 bat

Card game

Trace these shapes on to card. Colour the cards and cut them out. You will need four of each card. Use them to play Snap or Happy Families.

bat

owl

hedgehog

fox

badger

moth

November

Winter is coming and the sun is low in the sky. November days are often cold and misty and strong, wintry winds blow the last leaves from the trees.

People have made many changes to our native landscape. In the picture below, try to pick out at least twelve things which show that man has been here.

Answers on page 32.

Show that you care about wildlife and the countryside by making a badge with a suitable message and picture.

1   Cut out a circle of card 6 cm. across.
2   Write a slogan and draw a picture.
3   Using sticky tape, attach a safety pin to the back.

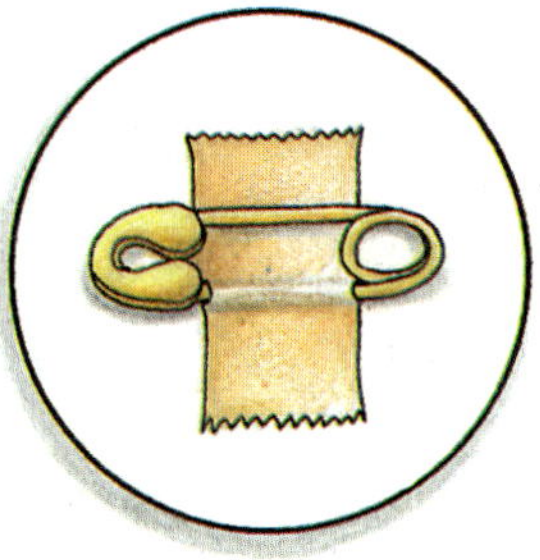

Design badges for your friends.

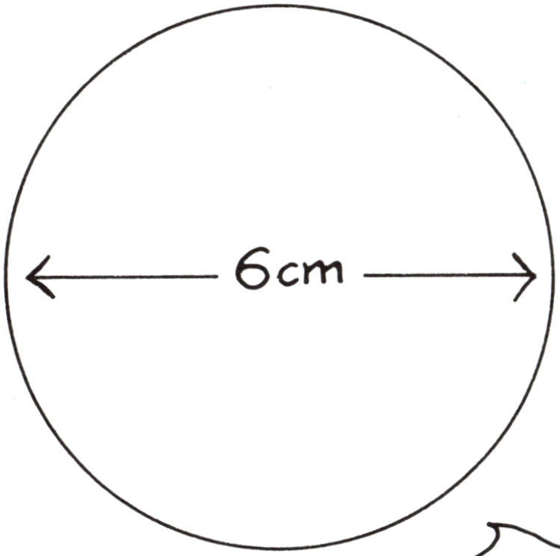

6cm

When should a mouse carry an umbrella?
When it's raining cats and dogs.

Do you know the countryside code? Follow this journey through the countryside and work out what the symbols mean.

Fasten all ⬜s.

Keep your 🐕s under close control.

Take your 🗑 home.

Guard against all risk of 🔥.

Keep to public 🌳 across farmland.

December

December has the shortest days and the longest nights. Winter is taking over and the countryside is still. The mammals have grown their winter coats and the birds fluff out their feathers to keep warm.

Cards to make

1 Fold a piece of card in half. (Make sure it's big enough for the picture you want to do.)

2 Trace an animal shape on to the card. Remember to have the fold in the right place. See below.

3 Colour and cut out.

4 Write the message inside.

make a woodland scene

fold

fold → LOUISE'S PLACE

HAPPY EASTER

fold

MERRY XMAS

fold

fold →

HAPPY MOTHER'S DAY
x x x x

Spider in the web

1 Trace the discs below on to firm card, keeping them joined in the middle.
2 Draw a spider on one half and a web on the other.
3 Glue them back to back.
4 Pierce holes.
5 Thread a piece of string 40 cm. long through each hole. Tie ends.
6 Twist ends quickly between your fingers and see the spider in his web.

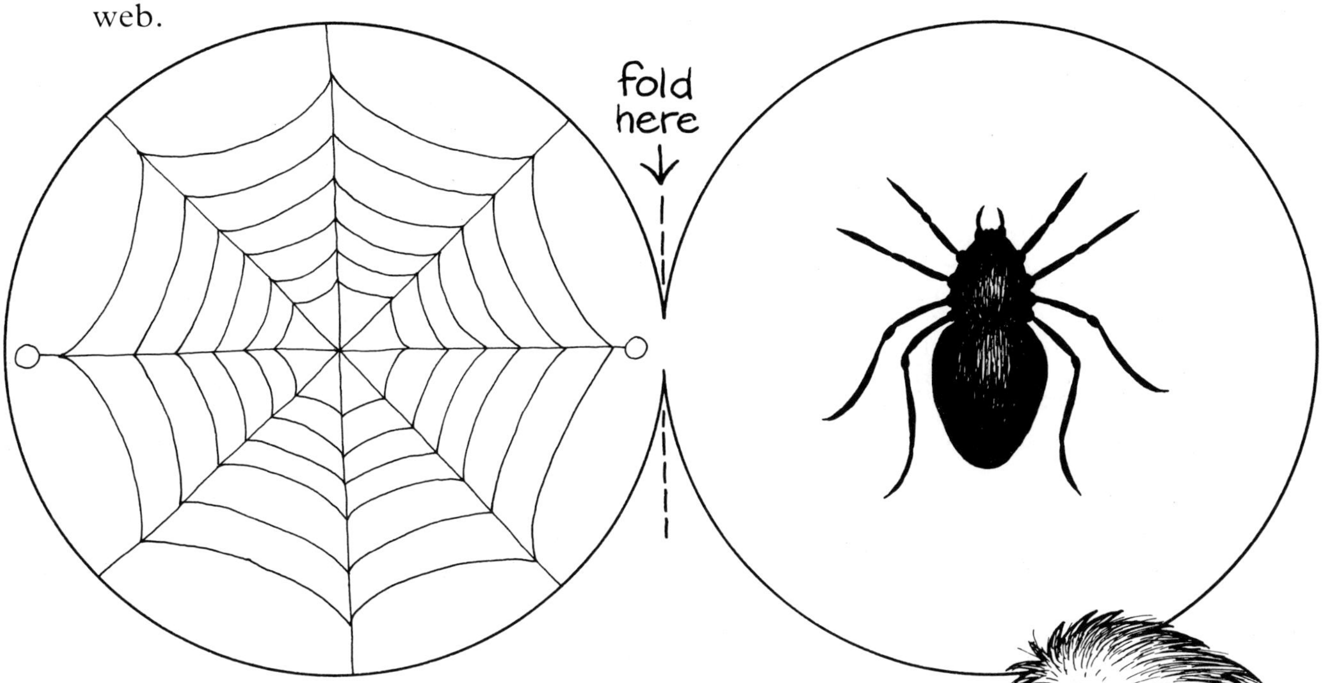

fold
here

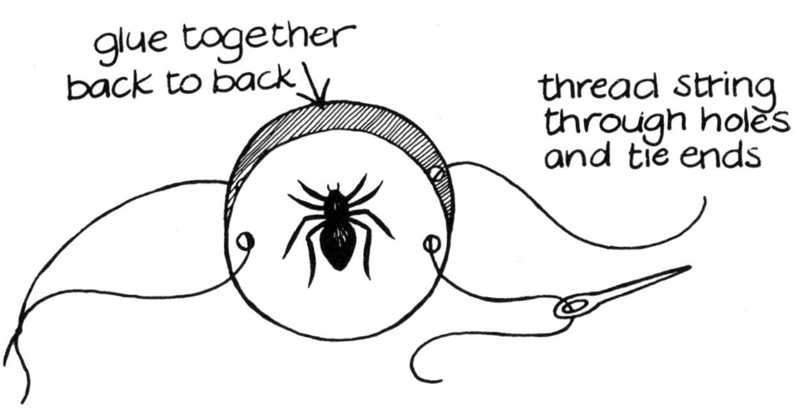

glue together
back to back

thread string
through holes
and tie ends

My Calendar

Trace the circles on to card, cut out and colour. Attach the circles using paper fasteners.

28

Make a daily weather record of your birthday month using these symbols.

 Cloudy

$////$ Rainy

Sunny

Snow and frost

1	2	3	4	5
6	7	8	9	10
11	12	13	14	15
16	17	18	19	20
21	22	23	24	25
26	27	28	29	30 / 31

Nature Quiz

See how many of these questions you can get right. *Answers on page 32.*

1 *Family matters.*

  a What animal has a billy for a father, a nanny for a mother and a kid for a baby?

  b What animal has a dog for a father, a vixen for a mother and a cub for a baby?

  c What animal has a stallion for a father, a mare for a mother and a foal for a baby?

2 *Which of these birds can't fly?* Kittiwake, kiwi, ostrich, peregrine, penguin, thrush and heron?

3 *Animals in books.* What kinds of animals are the following? Jeremy Fisher, Black Beauty, Tarka, Babar, Mog and Eeyore.

4 Can you identify these leaves from their silhouettes?

5 How many words can you make using the letters of the word

   HIPPOPOTAMUS

There are over fifty. Can you find that many?

6 Which animals are the odd ones out?
   Rabbit   badger   toad   sheep.
   Painted lady   tortoiseshell   cockroach   red admiral.
   Herring   trout   cod   dolphin.

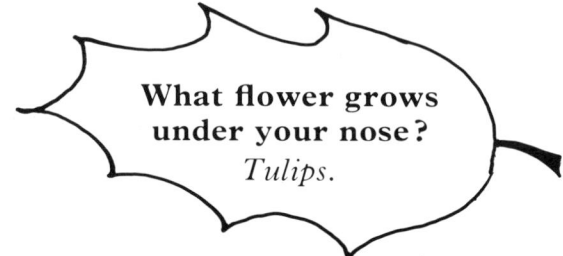

What flower grows under your nose?
Tulips.

7 Can you fill in the blanks with an animal from the list?

    a It's raining cats and . . . .   frog

    b A pretty kettle of . . . .   crow

    c A . . . . in the throat   hare

    d As the . . . . flies.   dogs

    e As mad as a March . . . .   fish

8 *Letter circles.* Each circle of letters makes the name of an animal or bird, written in either a clockwise or anti-clockwise direction. Can you work out what they all are?

    I P N O G E   G E R D A B   N I P F U F   W A S L U R

    S U P O O C T   A N H T P E L E   A L F M O G I N   G N I S L T A R

F	H	S	D	A	O	T
R	A	S	H	G	U	N
O	V	K	I	N	O	I
G	E	D	R	Y	T	K
S	H	A	V	E	S	S
O	M	S	T	F	O	T
O	T	H	M	O	I	S

9 FROGS HAVE SOFT SMOOTH MOIST SKIN, TOADS HAVE DRY TOUGH SKIN. Can you trace that round the letter maze starting at the arrow? Move one letter at a time either up or down or across (backwards and forwards). Use each letter once only and do not cross your path.

31

Quiz & Answers

Mighty Memory *Page 14*

1 What was the child in the pushchair pulling?
2 Where was the mole?
3 What were the pigeons doing?
4 How many magpies were there?
5 What was the boy on roller-skates eating?
6 What was the pattern on the ball?
7 What shape was the kite?
8 What was the girl with the dog doing?
9 Where was the squirrel?

Flower crossword *Page 12*

				R		
D	A	F	F	O	D	I	L
A				S			A
H		X		E			V
L		G					E
I		L					N
A		O	R	C	H	I	D
		V					E
V	I	O	L	E	T		R

Nature quiz *Pages 30 and 31*

1 *a* Goat, *b* fox, *c* horse.
2 Kiwi, ostrich, penguin.
3 Frog, horse, otter, elephant, cat, donkey.
4 Holly, horse-chestnut, oak, ash.
6 Toad, the rest are all mammals.
  Cockroach, the rest are all butterflies.
  Dolphins are mammals, the rest are fish.
7 *a* dogs, *b* fish, *c* frog, *d* crow, *e* hare, *f* mouse, *g* bull, *h* cat
8 Pigeon, badger, puffin, walrus.
  Octopus, elephant, flamingo, starling.

Spot the changes man has made *Page 24*

Aeroplane vapour trail/stone wall/gate/telegraph pole/lane/forest or orchard with trees in straight lines/hedge/tractor ruts/field with sheep/ruin of building/ploughed field/sawn down tree.

F	H	S	D	A	T	O	T
R	A	S	H	G	U	N	
O	V	K	I	N	O	I	
G	E	D	R	Y	T	K	
S	H	A	V	E	S	S	
O	M	S	T	F	O	T	
O	T	H	M	O	I	S	